Republ
Academies

Republican Academies

Rudolf Steiner on self-management, experiential study and self-education in the life of a college of teachers

EDITED BY
FRANCIS GLADSTONE

STEINER SCHOOLS FELLOWSHIP PUBLICATIONS

REPUBLICAN ACADEMIES: Rudolf Steiner on self-management, experiential study and self-education in the life of a college of teachers

Published by the
Steiner Schools Fellowship
Kidbrooke Park, Forest Row,
Sussex RH18 5JA, England

Designed by
NorthGate Publishers, Brighton,
and typeset in 10 point Bembo

Printed by
Terry Gearing
Forest Row, Sussex
on recycled paper

Cover illustration
Rudolf Steiner at a neolithic site during
a visit to Torquay, England, in 1924

CONTENTS

FOREWORD

As the twenty-first century approaches, the oldest Waldorf schools are venerable institutions in their seventies. This poses new challenges not met before. It is often observed that, in their early years, pioneer Waldorf schools have many of the strengths and difficulties of children and adolescents. Must the same principle apply to the oldest schools? Or is there some kind of alchemy by which their teaching and administration may be rejuvenated?

There will be no single answer appropriate to all ageing schools. Much will depend on the prevailing circumstances, each school's biography and the individual personalities carrying the work. But although there will be no right answer—only good, bad and indifferent ones—no strategy is likely to be adopted without some re-examination of the guidance provided by Rudolf Steiner during the founding phase of Waldorf education.

This is not an easy task. What Steiner said on the subject of college life and the management of Waldorf schools is scattered in many different places. So the first task has been to collate this material before going on to assess the relative weight given to different themes—a matter not easily ascertained from individual sources. When this is done it is evident that Steiner repeatedly returns to certain key issues when speaking of the role of the college of teachers in a Waldorf school.

The discrepancy between this vision and what often passes for college life leaves little room for complacency. Nevertheless, no attempt has been made to go on to prescribe any particular way of organising a Waldorf school. Addressing that challenge must remain the prerogative of those carrying each individual institution.

This study arose from discussions with colleagues at Michael Hall, an English Waldorf school founded in 1925. Its framework reflects that origin, to some extent, but because of interest expressed by colleagues in other Waldorf schools, both old and young, it is being made available more widely.

I am grateful to Richard Zienko and Ronald Jarman for helpful discussions over many years; to former colleagues at the South Devon Steiner School who helped me understand some of the central issues; to members of the college of teachers at Michael Hall School for inspiring me to re-examine Steiner's views on college life; to Martyn Rawson who read through an early draft and prompted some important changes; and to Alison Roberts and Christiana Bryan for proof-reading the final version. The many surviving shortcomings are, of course, entirely my responsibility.

Francis Gladstone
Forest Row, Sussex, Easter 1997

Part 1 Academies of Experiential Study

The real purpose of the college meetings is to study human development so that a real knowledge of human nature is continually flowing through the school *(Rudolf Steiner, Torquay, 19.8.1924)*

In the summer of 1924, the founding teachers of Michael Hall had the good fortune to receive a course of seven lectures during a conference at the seaside resort of Torquay. Published in English as *The Kingdom of Childhood,* these were the last lectures Steiner gave on the subject of education and, together with the lectures given in Oxford in 1922 and in Ilkley in 1923, they form a trilogy addressed to the English-speaking world.

At the end of the final lecture Steiner expressed his hope that the new venture would succeed in its aims, ending with the words, 'In conclusion I should like to give you my right good thoughts on your path—the path which is to lead to the founding of a school here on Anthroposophical lines'. This moment might be regarded as the inception of the college of teachers of Michael Hall. Certainly the timing of this lecture should not be ignored. It took place exactly five years after the first gathering of those who were to be the college of teachers in the first Waldorf school. This seems unlikely to have been accidental.

On the previous day (19 August 1924) Steiner had touched briefly on how a Waldorf school should be organised, ending with the words, 'These are the indications I wanted to give you for the practical organisation of your school'. His somewhat surprising starting point is the importance of cultivating fantasy.

> In the child between the change of teeth and puberty it is not the intellect but the fantasy that is predominantly active; we must constantly be thinking of the child's fantasy, and therefore, as I have often said, we must especially develop fantasy in ourselves . . . Fantasy can go astray, it is true, but it is rooted in reality, whereas the intellect remains always on the surface. That is why it is so infinitely important for the teacher himself to be in touch with reality as he stands in his class.

Steiner is not referring only to class-teachers here. Two years earlier, in the Oxford lectures, he had made it clear that upper school teachers must also work out of their imagination. He now goes on to link this task of teacher self-education to the tasks of the college meetings:

> In order that this may be so we have our college meetings in the Waldorf School which are the heart and soul of the whole teaching. In these meetings, each teacher speaks of what he himself has learnt in his class and from all the children in it, so that each one learns from the other. No school is really alive where this is not the most important thing, this regular meeting of the teachers . . . This is the real purpose of the college meetings, to study human development so that a real knowledge of the human being is continually flowing through the school. The whole school is the concern of the teachers in their meetings, and all else that is needed will follow of itself. The essential thing is that in the college meetings there is study, steady, continual study.

Many of the key issues about collegial working repeatedly stressed by Steiner are included in this brief statement. It may be useful to separate out four distinct themes:

1 *If a school is to be a living organism, the college of teachers must be its heart and soul*

2 *College study must start from teachers sharing their experience in the classroom [not from theory]. The chief purpose of the college meeting is to be a permanent teacher training 'academy'*

3 *Sharing classroom experience fosters unity, making the whole school the concern of each teacher*

4 *Through college study a real knowledge of human nature continuously flows out and permeates the school, bringing vitality to the work of the teachers*

Each of these themes had been more fully expounded on previous occasions and these earlier formulations may help to make clear exactly what Steiner had in mind.

1 If a school is to be a living organism, the college of teachers must be its heart and soul

A year earlier, in Ilkley, Steiner had stressed the importance of seeing schools as living organisms: 'I have said that a school ought to be an organism in which each single feature is an integral part of the whole. The threads of the different activities which must be carried on in order that the whole organism of the Waldorf School may live, are drawn together in the very frequent college meetings.' (17.8.23 *Modern Art* p 207). And the previous summer, in Oxford: 'The heart of the Waldorf School ... is the teachers' staff meeting ... Here, before the assembled staff, every teacher throughout the school will discuss the experiences he has in his class in all detail. Thus these constant staff meetings tend to make the school into an organism in the same way as the human body is an organism by virtue of its heart.' (23.8.22 *Spiritual Foundation* pp 93-4).

In short, just as blood from all parts of the body flows to the heart, so *experience* from all parts of the school must flow into the college meetings.

2 College study must start from teachers sharing their experience in the classroom [not from theory]. The chief purpose of the college meeting is to be a permanent teacher training 'academy'

Steiner repeatedly emphasised the importance of learning from experience. In the Oxford lectures, for instance, he compares a school with a medical patient:

> Hence also, there is no question of constructing the school on the lines of some bad invention—then indeed it would be a construction, not an organisation, but it is truly a case of studying week by week the organism that is there. Then an observer of human nature, and this includes child nature, will actually light upon the most concrete educational measures from month to month. As a doctor does not say at the very first examination everything that must be done for his patient, but needs to keep him under observation because the human being is an organism, so much the more in such an organism as a school must one make a continuous study. For it can very well happen that owing to the nature of the staff and children in 1920—say—one will proceed in a manner quite different from one's procedure with the staff and children one has in 1924. For it may be that the staff has increased and so quite changed, and the children will certainly be quite different. In face of this situation the neatest possible sections 1 to 12 would be of no use. Experience gained day by day in the classroom is the only thing that counts. (23.8.22 *Spiritual Foundation* pp 93–4).

And because of this central importance of experience, the college needs to become a kind of on-going teacher training seminar:

> These meetings are really the living 'High School' for the college of teachers—a permanent training academy, as it were. They are so indeed, and for the reason that every practical experience gained by the teacher in school becomes, in turn, part of his own education. And he who derives such self-education for himself from his teaching work, gaining on the one hand a profound psychological insight into the practical side of education and on the other into the different qualities, characters and temperaments of the children, will always be finding something new, for himself and for the whole college of teachers. All the experience and knowledge acquired from the teaching should be 'put into the pool' at these meetings. (Ilkley 17.8.23 *Modern Art* pp 207–8)

In Holland, a few weeks before the Torquay course, Steiner connects this 'learning from experience' with the absence of a head teacher in the Waldorf School—an absence never actually mentioned in the English lectures.

> Instead of a school director or head-master we have the college meetings, in which there is a common study and a common striving towards further progress. There is therefore a spirit, a concrete spirit living among the college of teachers which works freely, which is not tyrannical, which does not issue statements, rules or programmes, but has the will continually to progress, continually to make better and better arrangements, in meeting the teaching requirements. Today our teachers cannot know at all what will be good in the Waldorf School in five years time for in these five years they will have learned a great deal and out of the knowledge they will have to judge anew what is good and what is not good . . . Educational matters cannot be thought out intellectually, they can only arise out of teaching experience. And it is this working out of experience which is the concern of the college of teachers. (Arnhem 21.7.24 *Human Values* pp 92–3)

Related themes (a) The purpose of college study is to develop 'psychological perception'

Why Steiner does not refer to 'psychology' in the English context is unclear. On the continent of Europe he repeatedly emphasises its importance, not least in the preparatory seminar given in Stuttgart in the summer of 1919. The second lecture of *Study of Man,* which he says 'begins the study of education proper', opens with the words: 'In the future all teaching must be founded on a real psychology'. In the following days he returns many times to this theme; and in later years he relates 'psychology' to the role of the college. Lecturing at the Goetheanum in 1923, Steiner makes it clear that the way in which the collective study of classroom experience vitalises the teachers is by the development of 'a living and individualising psychology'.

> Yesterday I already mentioned that a united college of teachers, functioning like the soul and spirit of the entire school organism, is absolutely fundamental to the running of a Waldorf school. In accordance with one of its pedagogical impulses, it is not so much a statistical collation of the teachers' observations expressed during the meetings which matters, but that a living and individualising psychology should be jointly developed out of the actual experience of lessons taught . . . In the meetings of our college of teachers such matters as the proportion of boys to girls—and many other problems as well—are being worked through from a psychological and pneumatological aspect as part of a common study of soul and spirit. (Dornach 22.4.23 *Changing Consciousness* pp 178,193)

And this 'living and individualising psychology' cultivated in the college can vitalise the periphery—the life of the classroom—only if each and every teacher develops a capacity for psychological observation capable of providing a real understanding of each child:

> I should like to make clear first of all that the soul of all the instruction and education in the Waldorf School is the college meeting. These meetings are held regularly by the college of teachers and I attend them whenever I can manage to be in Stuttgart. They are concerned not only with external matters of school organisation, with the drawing up of the timetable, with the formation of classes and so on, but they deal in a penetrative, far-reaching way with everything on which the life and soul of the school depends. Things are arranged in such a way as to further the aim of the school, that is to say, to base the teaching and education on a knowledge of human development. It means of course that this knowledge must be applied to every individual child.

> Time must be devoted to the observation, the psychological observation of each child. This is essential and must be reckoned with in actual, concrete detail when building up the whole educational plan. In the teachers' meetings the individual child is spoken about in such a way that the teachers try to grasp the nature of the human being as such in its special relationship to the child in question . . . If we want to observe children in their real being we must acquire a psychological faculty of perception. (Arnhem 21.7.24 *Human Values* pp 92–3)

A cautionary note should be sounded here. At first sight these remarks could be taken to imply that every pupil should be the subject of child study in the college. But this would be completely unrealistic in all but the smallest of schools. What is really meant is that through college study of selected individuals the teachers shall develop the power to apply the same approach to all the children they teach.

Nor indeed should these remarks lead to an inordinate emphasis on individual child study at the expense of studying classes as a whole. The reference in the previous quotation to the effect of the proportion of girls in a class—dealt with in detail in several lecture courses—makes it clear that class studies and group psychology also need to be given adequate time.

Related themes (b) Developing psychological perception also needs 'width of interest'

The following day Steiner returns to the same theme, evidently anxious to stress the importance of cultivating 'width of interest' as a basis for 'psychological perception':

> Any teacher who enters lovingly into what is put forward here as the knowledge of human development will quickly acquire the possibility of observing each individual child with the attention that is necessary; and this they will be able to do even in a class where there are many pupils. It is just here however that the psychological perception of the kind which I have described is necessary, but this perception is not so easily acquired if one goes through the world as a single individual and has absolutely no interest in other people. I can truly say that I am aware of what I owe to the fact that I really never found any human being uninteresting. Even as a child no human being was ever uninteresting to me . . . It is this width of interest

> which permeates the college meetings at the Waldorf School and gives them atmosphere, so that—if I may so express myself—a psychological mood prevails throughout and these college meetings then really become a school based on the study of a deep psychology. It is interesting to see how from year to year the 'college of teachers' as a whole is able to deepen its faculty for psychological perception. (Arnhem 22.7.24 *Human Values* p 100)

Related themes (c) Colleagues should take an interest in each other's research

This width of interest, Steiner says, should also extend to the research work undertaken by colleagues, which may be more prevalent than appears at first sight:

> I would like to add one more thing to what I have already said, that will strike an anthroposophical note for you. I told you it would be good to get to know Baravalle's thesis. I would like to mention that, in any case, for basic occult reasons, it is of great importance for the enlivening of the teaching in all subjects if there is a lively interest taken in anything original produced by members of the college . . . This is extremely important; it enlivens the whole college of teachers if proper interest is taken in original work done by members . . . A programme ought to come out every year, and the whole college ought to be involved in it. It is really true that the spiritual forces of the college of teachers are carried by the sharing of inner scientific experience. Nothing must be closed off, there must be mutual co-operation. Here, where we come together, there is of course considerable mutual interest. There is the assumption that a lot more of you are producing original work on the quiet, so I would like to recommend that you let the others benefit from your work. (11.9.21 *Conferences* vol 2 p 38)

3 Sharing classroom experience fosters unity, making the whole school the concern of each teacher

Although Steiner never speaks about the absence of a head teacher in the lectures on education given in England, he did stress the importance of harmonious working in Oxford in 1922: 'Now what matters in these staff meetings is not so much the principles but the readiness of all teachers to live together in goodwill, and the abstention from any form of rivalry. And it matters supremely that a suggestion made to another teacher only proves helpful when one has the right love for every single child. And by this I do not mean the kind of love which is often spoken about, but the love which belongs to an artistic teacher.' (Oxford 23.8.22 *Spiritual Foundation* pp 93–4). And in Dornach, a year later, he insists that working in this way fosters unity:

> And so, in the educational system cultivated in the Waldorf School, the centre of gravity lies in the college of teachers and in their regular meetings, because the whole school is meant to be one living and spirit-permeated organism. Thus the teacher of Class I is expected to follow with real interest not only what the physics teacher is teaching to Class XII, but also the physics teacher's experiences of the various pupils in that class. All this flows together in the college meetings, where practical advice and counselling, based on actual teaching experience, are freely given and received. Through the college of teachers a real attempt is made to create a kind of soul for the entire school organism. And so the teacher of Class I will know that the teacher of Class VI has a child who is retarded in one way or another, or who may be an especially gifted child.
>
> Such common interest and shared knowledge have a fructifying influence. The entire teaching-body, being thus united, will experience the whole school as a unity. Then a common enthusiasm will pervade the school, but also a willingness to share in all its sorrows and worries. Then the entire teaching staff will carry whatever has to be carried, especially with regard to moral and religious issues, but also where matters of a more cognitive nature are concerned.
>
> In this way, the different colleagues will also learn how one particular subject, taught by one of the teachers, affects quite another subject, taught by another teacher. Just as, in the case of the human organism, it is not a matter of indifference whether the stomach is rightly adjusted to the head, so in a school it is not insignificant whether a lesson from nine to ten in the morning, given to Class III, is rightly related to the lesson from eleven to twelve in Class VIII. This is, of course, putting it in rather radical and extreme terms. Things do not happen quite like that, but they are presented in this way because they do correspond intrinsically to reality. (21.4.23 *Changing Consciousness* pp165–6)

4 Through college study a real knowledge of human nature continuously flows out and permeates the school, bringing vitality to the work of the teachers

Just as blood from the periphery flows into the heart, so experience in the classroom must flow into the college. The opposite movement—from the centre to the periphery—is only referred to once in detail. But the importance of this energising of the teachers' work is central to Steiner's picture of college life.

> In this way the college of teachers in spirit and soul becomes a whole where each member knows what the others are doing, what experience has taught them and what progress they have made as the result of their work with the children in the classroom. The college of teachers becomes, in effect, a central organ whence the whole life-blood of the practical teaching flows and helps the teacher to maintain his freshness and vitality. Probably the best effect of all is that these meetings enable the teachers to maintain their inner vitality instead of actually growing old in soul and spirit. It must be the teacher's constant aim to maintain a youthful freshness of soul and spirit, but this can only be done if true life-blood flows to a central organ, just as human blood flows to the heart, and out of it again. That is concentrated as a system of soul-spiritual forces in the life that is striven for in the college meetings at the Waldorf School. (Ilkley 17.8.23 *Modern Art* pp 207–8)

Experiential study and spiritual science

Clearly Steiner attached great importance to learning from *experience*. And there are many other occasions on which he stressed the importance of shaping teaching out of the concrete situation in which one finds oneself, and not out of theory:

> What teachers do can depend to only to a slight extent on what the general standards of abstract educational theory stimulate in them. It must rather be born anew, in each moment of their activity, out of their living understanding of the developing human being. ('The Pedagogical Basis of the Waldorf School', essay written in October 1919, in *Rudolf Steiner in the Waldorf School*, p 4)

He did not of course mean that there is no need to study spiritual science or the pedagogical lectures. Indeed it is evident that he was disappointed that the teachers tended to neglect such study. For example, when in 1922 a teacher asserted that 'problems accumulate because Dr. Steiner comes so seldom' he replied:

> Then we must invent a way of giving the year 975 days . . . I cannot come more often . . . I shall not consider the matter ripe for discussion until I see you studying what is already there. The pedagogical course you were given contains everything, only you need to study it . . .The material is completely ignored, it is just as if I had never given a seminar course here. (15.10.22 *Conferences* vol 3 p 11)

Nevertheless it seems clear that Steiner did not consider such study of the theory to be enough. The understanding of child development provided by spiritual science is the essential starting point, he says, but to learn how it can be creatively applied in the classroom requires continual sharing and discussion of classroom experience.

That adults learn much faster when new perspectives can be related to their own experience is much better understood today. The phenomenon has been repeatedly confirmed by educational research and the use of students' past and current experience as the starting point for their self-education is widespread in modern adult education. Experiential study is no longer a novel concept.

In sad contrast, Steiner's pioneering insight has all too often fallen on stony ground in the Waldorf schools themselves. Permanent teacher training 'academies' concentrating on 'experiential study' tend to be much rarer in the life of college than interminable, argumentative business meetings.

It may be that the four chief themes summarised in Torquay in 1924 are the most important in Steiner's conception of college life, especially, perhaps, for the group of teachers he was addressing and the school they were about to establish. But these four themes (together with the subsidiary issues also identified) by no means exhaust what he had to say on the subject and no account of Steiner's picture of the college would be adequate without examing the other issues he addressed.

Nevertheless it is important to point out that in all the many lectures given in England, none of these other issues was even mentioned which would seem to indicate that for some reason Steiner thought them relatively less important in the English context of the time.

Part 2 Republican Self-Management

The constitutional form given to the first Waldorf School is not among the themes to be found in the English lectures. But the Waldorf School's constitution cannot be regarded as something Steiner considered unimportant. It was the principal issue addressed on the first occasion he met with the future teachers of the original school. On the evening of 21 August 1919, welcoming them to the three week pedagogical seminar which began the following day, Steiner began by saying that, 'the Waldorf School must be taken as an opportunity to reform and revolutionise education'. (20.8.19 *Conferences* vol 1 p 34). All this was against the backdrop of a bold and ultimately unsuccessful attempt to promulgate a new, threefold ordering of the state as set out in *Towards Social Renewal* first published in 1919.

He did not promise the future Waldorf teachers an easy time: 'We shall have a hard fight, yet we have to carry out this cultural deed'. The main problem, he explained, was the strong tendency in modern societies for governments to interfere in education:

> The State will tell us how to teach and what results to aim for, and what the State prescribes will be bad. Its targets are the worst ones imaginable, yet it expects to get the best possible results. Today's politics work in the direction of regimentation, and it will go even further than this in its attempts to make people conform. Human beings will be treated like puppets on strings, and this will be regarded as progress in the extreme. Institutions like schools will be organised in the most arrogant and unsuitable manner. *(ibid)*

And although 'we shall need to make compromises' it was essential to resist this trend. One of the ways in which this should be done was to avoid the top-down, pyramidal organisational forms typical of most modern institutions:

> The school, therefore, will have its own management run on a republican basis and will not be managed from above. We must not lean back and rest securely on the orders of a headmaster; we must be a republic of teachers and kindle in ourselves the strength that will enable us to do what we have to do with full responsibility. Each one of you, as an individual, has to be fully responsible. *(ibid)*

Although a 'republic of teachers' was—and remains—a novel approach to the management of schools, it was not without precedent. The medieval universities were distinctly republican in character and in England the colleges of Oxford and Cambridge have preserved a version of this form of self-management. The danger of such an arrangement is that each member of the 'republic' goes his or her own way so that the school lacks any unity of approach. But according to Steiner this danger can be avoided if the teachers share a common understanding of the task in hand:

> We will replace the duties of a headmaster by having this preparatory seminar in which we will work to acquire the spirit that will unite the school. If we work hard, this seminar will engender in us our spirit of unity. *(ibid)*

Steiner's rejection of monarchical forms of governance was reiterated and further explained on subsequent occasions. At the close of the three week seminar he states that, 'College meetings are republican conversations in which all the teachers are their own masters.' (8.9.19 *Conferences* vol 1 p 38). And eighteen months later, when discussing a proposed biennial report, he remarked that 'You ought to make a strong point of the freedom of the college with its republican-democratic organisation in order to show that even with our limited possibilities a free spiritual life is possible.' (16.1.21 *Conferences* vol 2 p 10).

A few days earlier, when addressing a parents evening, Steiner had given a more detailed account of why a republican constitution was needed. It is necessary, he explains, in order to preserve the direct connection with free spiritual activity essential if teachers are to remain flexible and modify their approach in the light of experience:

> All instruction must be pervaded by a specific educational principle that can be attained only if the teachers themselves are fully involved in spiritual activity. It is not possible for them to do this if they are not aware of their responsibility to the spiritual life. However, ladies and gentlemen, it is only possible to take up this great responsibility toward the spiritual life if it is not being replaced for us by a merely external feeling of responsibility. If we proceed simply according to what is prescribed for a single school year, we feel relieved of the need to research week by week both what we are to take up in school with regard to the individual subject, and how we are to present it.

It should be characteristic of our teachers that they draw again and again from the living spiritual source. In doing so, they must feel responsible to the spiritual life and know that the spiritual life is free and independent. The school must be self-managing; teachers cannot be civil servants.

They must be fully their own masters, because they know a higher master than any outer circumstance, the spiritual life itself, to whom they stand in a direct connection that is not mediated by school officials, principals, inspectors, school boards, and so forth. The activity of teaching, if it is really independent, requires this direct connection to the sources of spiritual life. Only teachers who possess this direct connection are then able to convey the spiritual source to the children in their classes . . .

In the time since we began our work, we have carefully reviewed from month to month how our principles are working with the children. In the years to come, some things will be carried out in line with different or more complete points of view than in previous years. This is how we would like to govern this school—out of an activity that is direct and unmediated, as indeed it must be if it flows from spiritual depths. (13.1.21, *Rudolf Steiner in the Waldorf School* pp 77-9)

Practical aspects of republican self-management

Shortly after this Steiner visited Holland and, in a lecture given in the Hague, addressed some of the practical aspects of what is entailed by republican self-management:

One of the demands that must be made for spiritual life—something that is not at all utopian, that may be begun any day—is that those actively engaged in spiritual life (and this means, above all, those involved in its most important public domain; namely, education) should also be entrusted with all management matters, and this in a broad and comprehensive way.

The maximum number of lessons to be taught—plus the hours spent on other educational commitments—should allow teachers sufficient time for regular meetings, in both smaller and larger groups, to deal with management matters.

However, only practising teachers—not former teachers now holding state positions or retired teachers—should be called on to care

> for this side of education. For what has to be administered in each particular school—as in all institutions belonging to the spiritual-cultural life—should be only a continuation of what is being taught, of what forms the content of every word spoken and every deed performed in the classroom.
>
> Rules and regulations must not be imposed from outside the school. In spiritual life, autonomy, self-management, is essential. (27.2.21 *Education and Anthroposophy,* p 52)

Membership of the college of teachers—an 'intimate college'?

The question of membership of the college of teachers had already been discussed during the previous year with the teachers in Stuttgart:

> It cannot be taken for granted that all the specialist teachers should be on the college. There ought to be an intimate college consisting of class teachers and the older specialist teachers, and also a larger college . . . Only the principal teachers belong on the college, and those among them who are actually teaching, not those on leave of absence. Basically the ones on the college should be those who have been at the school since the beginning, and among the teachers who came later those whom we would have wished to have at last year's course. Whoever joins us as a genuine teacher has always been considered. To be on the college they must in the first place be actually teaching and secondly they must be real teachers. (30.7.20 *Conferences* vol 1 p 114)

However, there was an exception to this general rule. Although not a teacher, the businessman Emil Molt attended college meetings throughout the early years. This was partly in deference to the crucial role he had played in the founding of the school. But it seems likely that it was also because his outstanding entrepreneurial skills made a critical contribution to the school's continuing growth and success. There is a significant precedent here for the presence in the college of a non-teacher with particular expertise, albeit one deeply versed in the anthroposophical basis of the education.

Decisions about the timetable and the appointment of new teachers

The nature of the task of the college of teachers, and the primary emphasis on 'experiential study' has already been discussed in part 1. But brief mention must be made of two other topics which Steiner saw as needing to be brought to college meetings. In 1922 he stated that, 'The timetable ought to be decided in the conference' (15.10.22 *Conferences* vol 3 p 5). And in 1920 he says the appointment of new teachers ought to be discussed in the college:

> I also beg you to remember that the nominating of new teachers has always been discussed in the college of teachers. I should like to keep it this way. I think that ideals must at least play a part, and that it ought to be like this: that the college of teachers anticipates that we make the nomination with a certain amount of penetration and take our decision very seriously. I would always report what has happened. I would never exclude the consideration of proposals made from the other quarter. (21.9.20 *Conferences* vol 1 p 118)

But exactly what this means is unclear. It could imply that while the college should be consulted about appointments, the decision was to be made by Steiner himself. But it could be interpreted to imply that the decision was to be made in the college.

Republican not democratic: the empowerment of mandates

During the fourth year of the Waldorf School a number of difficulties with the republican form became apparent. But before turning to how Steiner dealt with what can only be described as a management crisis, some further comments on republican self-management may be useful. Of particular interest is a short essay entitled *Republican not Democratic* in which Ernst Lehrs, one of the first Waldorf teachers, contributed some invaluable insights into what is needed for successful self-management.

Concentrating on the management tasks to be carried out by teachers in addition to their pedagogical activity, Lehrs stresses that the republican approach cannot be reconciled with a reluctance to *empower* the teachers concerned. The assignment of a *mandate* to take responsibility for a particular management task is a decision to be taken by the college of teachers; it is essentially a democratic matter although the members of college need to take into account the suitability of particular individuals for the work involved. But once the mandate has been given, college members need to empower the mandate holder by accepting and supporting the decisions he or she reaches, even if they disagree with them. On the other hand, the mandate holder must consult all those likely to be affected before reaching a decision and give them the opportunity to put their point of view. And where mandate holders are felt not to have discharged their duties adequately, it is open to the college to decide not to renew the mandate when the holder's term of office comes to an end—or, in extreme cases, to terminate the mandate prematurely.

Between monarchism and collectivism: the republican way

The republican mandate is essentially an aristocratic form, albeit one which is time-limited, and the problem that arises over and over again is that teachers in Waldorf schools fail to resist the temptation to challenge the decisions made by mandate holders. But when this happens republican self-management is severely weakened and individuals become unwilling to take on such responsibilities.

Quite often this arises from a confusion between the republican approach and what might be called 'democratic collectivism', a form of self-government in which everybody votes on every significant decision, or where everyone must agree before any decision can be reached (consensus decision-making). The attraction of 'collectivism' often originates from people's painful experience of the oppressive behaviour of authoritarian power holders. Indeed, experience of oppression in early life may be among the reasons some people are attracted to work in Waldorf schools. Certainly the resentment caused by experiences of oppression often engenders a deep distrust of any form of power.

And this is a profound challenge of self-development. Because the difficulty with the 'collectivist' approach is that at best decision-making soon becomes extremely constipated; while at worst it degenerates into mob rule. Certainly there is ample evidence from sociological research that most such 'collectives' fail to thrive and develop, and many are very short-lived.

Republican self-management is a middle way between 'collectivism' and traditional monarchical, authoritarian forms of governance which depends on members of the 'republic' being prepared to empower some of their number to reach decisions on their behalf.

It is important, too, to recognise that teaching tasks are also a form of republican mandate—indeed, in the case of schools, they are the primary mandates. Individual teachers must be free to make their own decisions about how to teach. This is not to say they should be unaccountable. They should regularly bring their experience to the college (as described earlier, p 4) and be prepared to listen to others' opinions about the approach they are taking. But they must remain 'their own masters'.

Part 3 Republicanism and Social harmony

The merit of the republican approach is that it secures individual freedom, a necessary condition for creative work. Its danger, as already said, is that the members of the republic fail to use that freedom to work together towards a common end. And when the give and take of free co-operation is absent, social harmony evaporates and unity is lost.

Steiner had hoped (see p 12) that what was given in the preparatory seminar of 1919, together with the continued sharing of experience in the college meetings—would lead to mutual support and an *esprit de corps* which would counteract this danger. But he was destined to be disappointed.

The teaching lacks fire

During a visit made in the autumn of 1922, shortly after the beginning of the fourth school year, Steiner begins to express serious concern about the state of the school. Some of what he has seen has pleased him but overall he is concerned that the 'good principles' of Waldorf school education are no longer being applied adequately. He does not mince his words:

> Steiner: We shall naturally suffer the consequences if what is good in principle becomes bad through being badly applied. What is good must be made good use of. What we need is some enthusiasm, some inner activity. That has gradually disappeared. Only the lower classes are still active, and they make a frightful noise! This lifeless way of teaching, this indifference with which a lesson is given, without any impetus, has to be overcome. Some things are excellent, as I have already told the respective individuals. In other places there is the merest smattering of what should be there. We need vitality in the lessons, real vitality; that will pull things together . . . Many of you seem to work on the principle that you do not need to prepare your lessons any more . . .
>
> If only we had a guarantee that you people will realise once more that you have to follow the Waldorf school principles. If only we had a guarantee of that! But I see no sign of it . . . I miss the fire which

ought to be in it. There is not fire but apathy. There is a certain laziness there. Our original intentions hardly come to expression at all.

A teacher: I want to go.

Steiner: I do not want to arouse any ill-feeling. That is not the point. If I thought things were not improving I would have to speak differently. I always take it for granted that the college consists of people who have ability. I am convinced that the system is to blame. But people are asleep and function as though their eyes and ears were shut. I am not reproaching a single teacher, but routine methods are gaining ground. There is no hard work, but that could be changed. Hard work is what is lacking. (15.10.22 *Conferences* vol 3 pp 3–4)

The teachers are drifting apart

All this he says 'must be partly due to the atmosphere caused by having lost contact with one another' and later he returns to this lack of contact: 'You mustn't be angry if I say that the college of teachers is a heavy, solid body, firmly installed on lofty seats. We shall go to the dogs that way. The worst is yet to come.' (*ibid* pp 11–12). And he brushes aside a teacher's plea to take into account the difficulties caused by bad housing conditions.

That is certainly very important. Yet if I wanted to make an accusation I could object otherwise. It does not alter the fact that the school is as it is. It makes no difference at all. I do not want to accuse anyone I just want to say that this is how things are. It is awfully difficult. I have said so much that sticks in the gullet. It comes of knowing that things have to change

For instance the matter of there being no contact between you doesn't have anything to do with the housing question, does it? The fact that each one goes his own way is connected with the state of the school . . . Each one shuts himself up in his own four walls and it will soon reach the point when you don't even know each other any more. This has gradually been getting worse.

What one person does must flow over into the others into the forces of the group. There must be joyful appreciation of individual achievements. There is not the goodwill. There is no joyful appreciation of one another's performance. Individual achievements are ignored . . . If I work and nothing happens, it is crippling. Negative criticism is only justified if accompanied by positive criticism. There is indifference with regard to positive achievements. People become stultified if nobody takes a scrap of notice of what they achieve. (*ibid* pp 11-12)

Social harmony depends on humility and self-control

A term later Steiner remains worried about the lack of social harmony. Instead of falling into factions, the members of college should strive to make it a 'model of harmonious co-operation'. And this requires humility. The path of self-knowledge challenges us to work on recognising our own shortcomings rather than focusing on others' faults:

> I am sorry that the harmonious atmosphere has been broken . . . Unless a kind of self-discipline makes its appearance, we cannot progress. It pains me that it is like this; not to mention the fact that I cannot discover what this is all supposed to be about, it is like groping in the dark. If things were satisfactory in a particular direction, but to grope in the dark—I don't know what you had in mind.
>
> There is such a mood of tension here. It is really about time you started thinking. It should be the duty of the Waldorf teachers to end this sloppiness. This is one of your bad methods, to do things like this. It is really too bad about today's conference. It cannot help but bring disharmony, can it?
>
> . . . New things are being expected of us all the time. The Waldorf School could contribute a lot to this, if the college of teachers were to present a model of harmonious co-operation. Each one of you must really make his own contribution to this. That is where individual work comes into consideration; each individual should start to brighten his own work up. It is a Philistine attitude only to look for other people's faults. (17.1.23 *Conferences* vol 3 pp 54–5)

And during the next three weeks, while patiently facilitating a management reorganisation, he repeatedly returns to the subject of group harmony.

> The Waldorf School can only thrive if the college is harmonious. It is not possible that each of you will like all the others equally well, but that is your own private affair, and it does not belong in college. But in so far as the college represents the whole Waldorf School then the school's welfare depends on the inner harmony of the college.

There is a great difference between someone in the outside world telling somebody 'that gets on my nerves', and saying the same words here in a conference. In a college meeting and in the whole management of the Waldorf School there are only Waldorf School teachers, and the difficulties arise only because of our usual democratic running of the school. Of course there are difficulties. But I object to the words being used in college 'two levels of responsibility'. That could be the beginning of something very bad, if things like two levels of responsibility and the forming of cliques among college members form part of our discussion. Such things must be strictly excluded. (23.1.23 *Conferences* vol 3 p 61-3)

Is it really impossible for people to tell one another 'I have this and that against you', without liking one another any the less for it, or working any less willingly together? Why shouldn't you speak the truth directly and still appreciate and respect one another? (31.1.23 *Conferences* vol 3 pp 64–69)

Social harmony needs warmth, positivity . . . and picnics

By the spring of 1923 Steiner is becoming less concerned about the quality of the teaching. But he remains worried about the quality of relationships:

One can now really say that apart from exceptional circumstances and details that can be improved upon, the teaching has become satisfactory again; it has very much improved. On the other hand a certain coldness, chilliness is there among the college of teachers particularly where relationships are concerned. And the college meetings will only produce dissension if this chilliness becomes too great. You should really make every effort, mutually, to overcome this.

When you say you cannot get to know one another in college meetings, it seems odd to me that in a community that is always together from morning till evening, meets in every break and has the chance, every break, of smiling at one another, talking in a friendly way and having warm exchanges, that has so many opportunities to get things going, I cannot understand why you cannot manage it without having recourse to the college meetings. In the college you give each other the very best you can.

The trouble is that you ignore one another too much in college, and you do not smile at one another enough. Now and again you

> can tell one another the blunt truth, that helps the digestion and does no harm, if it is done in the right place. But you must behave to one another in such a way that each one of you knows that the other one does not only feel that way about you because he likes or dislikes you but because you are Waldorf teachers together . . . I see too many sour faces. This is something we must watch . . .
>
> I was dumbfounded when people spoke about dissension at the college meetings, as this means there must be some discord or at least indifference among you. I cannot understand why you don't feel how mighty glad you are when you can sit down with all the other Waldorf teachers. The right mood would be, 'It is a week now since we had a college meeting and I am overjoyed that I can foregather with them all again'. When one sees that this is not so, one is dumbfounded.
>
> It would certainly be lovely if the teachers were to have a kind of picnic together every so often. (6.2.23 *Conferences* vol 3 pp 80–1)

What the individual can do to improve college meetings

Steiner insists that personal disagreements do not belong in college life: 'There cannot be such a thing as a Waldorf teacher who is not well disposed towards another Waldorf teacher. There is no need to thrash out questions of conscience in front of the whole assembly. As members of the college you can sort it out on an individual basis. It could all be done perfectly tactfully.' *(ibid)* And when he is asked what can be done so that 'good impulses come to expression' in the meetings he replies:

> Isn't it the same thing here as anywhere, that actually the one who is dissatisfied with the meetings or whatever, can do a lot to improve them by making a personal effort to that effect in the actual college meeting itself? If the college meeting strikes you as too bad, can't you try to make it as good as possible? If you yourself find that it weighs you down so much that you have to throw it off after the conference, things will improve if you behave in the sort of way that makes others feel happy by the time they leave.
>
> You should not come to the college meeting with the idea of what you can get out of it but rather what you can put into it. It is not the criticism that is valuable but the attempts to improve the thing itself . . .

Individually you should look on the college meetings as something that you should help to make as stimulating as possible for everyone, so that there is no reason for anyone to grumble. If it does occur to someone to complain, he ought to think: What must *I* do, damn it, to make things better next time?' (*ibid*)

In short, republican social harmony presupposes that members of the republic—whether by following Steiner's suggestions for self-education or in other ways—are making progress towards the qualities striven for in the so-called *'supplementary exercises'* first described in *Knowledge of the Higher Worlds*: equanimity, positivity, open-mindedness and self-control.

PART 4 FORMATION OF A MANAGEMENT COUNCIL

The loss of social harmony arising from lack of social skills was not the only problem Steiner addressed at this time. For it had become apparent that the college meetings were becoming swamped by management matters. To redress this problem Steiner endorses the proposal that responsibility for the running of the school should be separated out from the college meetings. But to preserve the republican approach this responsibility should be shared by a small committee of three or four people.

> For quite a long time now I have been hearing from all sides that the mood of the college desired this sort of arrangement. With these impressions as my basis I answered any enquiries on the matter by saying that I believed it was necessary. It gives me a certain satisfaction to see it actually happening in this way, but I also think it really had to happen. (23.1.23 *Conferences* vol 3 pp 61-3)

Steiner outlines the proposed new arrangements and urges the teachers to be frank in sharing their view of the matter:

> That is a painful chapter, and as such I have given a great deal of thought to it. The reason why it is painful is because we can only really carry out our intentions if it is done in accordance with the will of the whole college, or at least a large majority. On the other hand, of course, the way it should be organised will have a strong effect on the way it will be accepted
>
> First of all I want you to bear in mind what has to be included in this new management organisation. For there is a great deal of

current business which obviously has to be done by the person in the school house. These things connected with the person in the house must be excluded.

Regarding everything that concerns the management which at the same time represents the school in the outside world, it would be advisable in future to have a small committee of three or four people instead of one. This group will only be able to work in rotation, so they will take it in turns to do the work, and only confer together about important matters or things that warrant being dealt with jointly. We should certainly have a committee of this kind so that our republican arrangements are not violated.

May I now ask any of you who have something to say on this matter to express yourselves frankly. Even if you want to say something you think most people will disapprove of, please speak up. (*ibid*)

One of the teachers pointed out that that a pure rotation of office did not take account of differing skills: 'There are certain things we know only Mr Y can do, and there are certain things that other people could do better'. Steiner accepts the argument and extends it:

I thought that if there is a committee there will be constant representation through the fact that its members take it in turns to carry out specified tasks. What you have just said can be done in that whichever member of the committee is considered the most capable person to do a particular job is designated by one or both of the others . . . It can be thought out even further. Let us have this committee and let the whole college agree that if this committee thinks that a particular member of the college of teachers should be designated to do a certain job, they should go ahead. (*ibid*)

In other words teachers may be appointed to non-teaching mandates by the 'management council'. He goes on to suggest that the planning of college meetings should be taken on by the new council:

Preparing the college meeting can also be the job of the respective committee member. This will make his task rather a difficult one. Preparing for the college meeting can certainly be among the tasks of whichever committee member is in charge of the running of the school at the time. The important thing is that this is one in complete harmony with the whole college. (*ibid*)

This proves uncontentious and Steiner goes on to enquire whether a committee of seven teachers which had been formed to deal with certain questions arising out of the Anthroposophical Society might take responsibility for preparing a detailed proposal.

> I wanted to ask the burning question as to whether this group enjoys sufficient confidence of the college of teachers to make proposals for a definite arrangement. We can discuss what the definite arrangement should be. It would be difficult for us today to come to any conclusions, as the idea has only just been born. As I shall presumably have to be here again soon, it would be better if today we were to answer the question, Does this group, or an extended group, have the confidence of the whole college to such an extent that it could make proposals for the planning of the next conference?'. . . It is more complicated to deal with this question at college than to have it dealt with by a group which has the confidence of the college. (*ibid*)

It rapidly became evident that this group was not universally trusted and that some members of the college felt it was a clique. Steiner, responded sharply, obviously troubled by the surfacing of factionalism:

> The Waldorf School can only thrive if the college is harmonious. It is not possible that each of you will like all the others equally well, but that is your own private affair, and it does not belong in college. But in so far as the college represents the whole Waldorf School then the school's welfare depends on the inner harmony of the college. There is a great difference between someone in the outside world telling somebody 'that gets on my nerves', and saying the same words here in a college meeting . . . When words like that slip out you could not say that there are even the very first beginnings of a college of teachers. (*ibid*)

But it soon became obvious that the attitudes expressed were deeply held and Steiner realised that a different solution was needed. He also ruled out choosing the preparatory group himself:

> Certain things have been said which have not been taken back. So we may assume that the arrangement will not be a success if we do it the way we originally intended. I could equally well imagine that in the light of the impulses on which the school and the teaching staff are based, in a matter like this I could choose a group. But I will not

do it because it is evident that there are certain suspicions. I would like to wait before doing such a thing until matters are cleared up. There are such antagonisms. (*ibid*)

The work of a preparatory committee should not be swept aside

Instead he had a preparatory committee of six members chosen by secret ballot and asked them to 'study these things in order to make proposals about management and 'to propose individuals who will do the job'. A week later this committee presented its proposals. (31.1.23 *Conferences* vol 3 pp 64–69)

> A teacher: The committee chosen at the last college meeting has proposed three teachers to run the school management in collaboration with the previous school administrators. These three would deputise in all school affairs, internal and external, with the exception of house administration, office and finances. The internal school affairs they will take over are:
>
> 1. Preparing for and minuting of the college meetings;
> 2. Co-opting individual colleagues for definite jobs, ie the allotting of living quarters. Decorating classrooms;
> 3. The setting up and maintaining of a plan of supervision;
> 4. Distribution and arrangement of classrooms;
> 5. Supervising the letting of schoolrooms for outside events.
>
> The external school affairs they will take over are:
>
> 1. Corresponding and dealing with the authorities. Countersigning of all the relevant documents.
> 2. Everything to do with pupils' admission (introducing tests) and leaving (dealing with reports);
> 3. Annual reports;
> 4. Receiving visitors;
> 5. Propaganda articles: consulting with the Association for Independent Spiritual life in our fight against the primary school law; collecting data for control of salaries; administration of special donations.
>
> Those would be the various jurisdictions contained in the present management which could be tackled by a corporate body.

Steiner then proposes that they begin by discussing 'the principle of the matter. I should like to ask you to say how far you agree or disagree, or whether you have anything at all to say on the matter?' No one, it seems, had much to say about the principle and the discussion turned to a proposal that a fourth individual should be added to the three the committee had nominated. Steiner is not at all happy with this; to him it represents a vote of no confidence in the committee.

> The path we took was to give the matter to a preliminary committee to investigate, as we assume that such a committee makes better proposals than people who make them straight out of their heads. The practice must be established more and more that we accustom ourselves to speak out of a sense of responsibility. The point now is that this committee has recently been chosen. We assume that it makes its proposals on a basis of mature consideration and responsibility . . . In itself, of course, it is not a vote of no confidence in the committee if the four gentlemen are chosen. But the whole treatment of the matter would be a no confidence vote because you threw the committee's proposal to the winds without any discussion. *(ibid)*

After much further discussion the proposal to enlarge the management council was withdrawn and a vote taken to appoint the members recommended by the preparatory committee. Then Steiner had the college members vote on the details of the proposed mandate before going on to the question of how long the term of office should be, and the rotation of duties. A relatively long spell of duty was proposed—two to three months—on the grounds that otherwise the continuity would constantly be interrupted. Steiner was keen that the term of office should not be too long. 'I think a term office of two months is appropriate, don't you? We have to watch that it does not become a burden'. *(ibid)*

College life under new management

The following week the newly-appointed officiating member of the administrative council proposed a fresh approach to the college meetings:

> It seems to me that it is important we aim for a new focus for our college meetings. There should not be anyone here who thinks these college meetings are not necessary. The apathy with which we have been coming to college meetings up till now must disappear. I think that right from the beginning of a college meeting we should have a mood which lends importance to it. I believe we can restore to the

college meetings something which used to be present to a far greater degree whilst we still retained the atmosphere of our first beginnings. This is not a new idea of mine. We shall try not to bring management matters to the conference. (6.2.23 *Conferences* vol 3 pp 80–1)

Continuing problems: experiential study cannot be a class thirteen

Sad to relate, this attempt to renew the original impulse for college working was not entirely successful. Some eight months later it proved necessary to return to the subject of the work of college. The discussion (16.10.23 *Conferences* vol 4 pp 54-6) is worth including in full:

Steiner: What I have especially on my mind—and what I would ask you to discuss first—are all the circumstances connected with a shattering letter I have had from Mr X telling me he wants to withdraw from the administrative group. He does not seem to possess a sufficient amount of the confidence he assumes should exist between the college and himself.

I know that the college has asked him to take back his decision, but I have already told him that it is—that in our college it is not just the superficial relationships that have to be sound but the whole foundations of our working together. We cannot possibly work in the way I described in the lecture we have just had (Lecture 3 of *Deeper Insights*) if the basic relations among the college are not sound, and not everybody works with, also into and from out of, everyone else. This must be cultivated more and more in our school.

When one goes into a teacher's lesson one must always know and feel what the others are doing. Sometimes I go into one or another lesson and, I must say, some things would not be as they are if the sort of thing were being done in other lessons which should be having its effect in this one. It is so important to work together, and the impulse must come from the meetings. If each one of us were to go his own way and work regardless of the others, we should not be capable of fulfilling our task. Therefore I do not see this as a solution. And I should like to press all of you who are involved in any way to give your frank opinion about what has been going on more behind the scenes than on the surface.

Mr X: In my opinion it is not so much me personally as the job that is to blame for undermining people's confidence. It would be good if something came about that would really guarantee progress. That would be more important than the part of it that relates to me.

A teacher: Mr X has told us that meetings were not as he would have wished. He believed he had not succeeded in giving the meetings a living form. But none of us could have done it. The increase in staff numbers makes things rather cumbersome.

Steiner: I don't quite see why enthusiasm should decrease as staff numbers increase. It would be sad if that were so. New teachers should be new sources of enthusiasm. If you want a room to be brighter you light more lamps not extinguish them. Serious things have been happening.

A number of people: Not at all!

Steiner: But my dear friends, surely a resignation like this must have serious reasons. It cannot be the case that nothing serious has happened. We ought to take these things seriously.

A teacher: As a matter of fact I have lost confidence in the college's will to co-operate in the meetings. The way they have been going, I had to give my blessing to someone who stayed away because the meetings were not achieving anything.

A teacher: Mr X ought to tell us why the meetings do not satisfy him.

Steiner: I should also like to ask in what way the meetings are unsatisfactory.

Several teachers spoke of incidents that had occurred.

Steiner: The kind of things you are bringing up are either discussed or they are not. One way of doing it is to shake one's head like people are doing in Fraulein A's corner. But if you do discuss things it shows that after all you do feel co-operative. It really would be good if we could talk about reasons why things like this are being discussed at all. I do think that on a superficial level it is just misunderstandings. But these arise, of course, out of the 'fors' and 'againsts'.

A teacher: I have tried to build up a picture. Out of a sense of responsibility Mr X wants to train the college to have a certain discipline. For reasons of temperament this has led to misunderstandings.

Steiner: You have touched on something that I would gladly discuss with you. It was already mentioned in my lecture today that one has to find a way despite the temperaments; There was the endeavour, despite the temperaments, to come to inner understanding. I should like to hear how this misunderstanding between the temperaments arose. If I pinpoint what you are actually saying, Mr Y, it is that Mr X wanted to turn the college of teachers into a class 13. The college wouldn't have it and rebelled against being subjected to education *[ie they felt treated like children: the highest class in the school was class 12]*.

A teacher: Reported on incidents that were at the root of it.

Steiner: As I cannot regard these things as anything else but a lighted match dropping into a barrel of gunpowder, I should like to hear more about the causes than about the incidents. (Reports were given). This brings the problem to light but does not solve it. Mr X resigned at the end of his tour of duty. Over the next four months the other two are due to hold office. Do we have to live with a thorn in our flesh just now when times are so difficult? For that is what a resignation amounts to . . .

Steiner: In my opinion the business about class 13, which a number of you confirmed, has something to do with it.

A teacher: People are determined, despite class 13, to have confidence in Mr X . . .

Steiner: Having listened to more discussion I still think there are things behind this. I understand neither the objective beginning nor how it can lead to resignation. It is bound to have to do with personal matters that cannot be brought forward here because we ought to remain objective.

Mr X was asked to continue in office, and he accepted. The published *Conferences* are silent on how far the Stuttgart college of teachers succeeded in making college life the harmonious, vitalising 'heart and soul' of the school that Steiner had hoped for. But it is well known that many Waldorf schools have found this ideal difficult to achieve.

Part 5 Objective Spirit

Love does not govern but it shapes and that is more (Goethe: Fairy Story)

The new approach to republican self-management and the emphasis on the self-education needed for social harmony were not the only ways in which Steiner tried to heal the crisis in the Stuttgart Waldorf School. At the beginning of 1923 he also created a new ceremony for the teachers and oldest pupils, the *Offering Service.* Those who attend this service have the opportunity to welcome the spirit of Christ into their lives and there can be little doubt that Steiner saw this as a third way in which the crisis could be overcome.

Because a ceremony was how the Waldorf School began its work. On the evening of 20 August 1919 the teachers gather for the first time. Welcoming them, Steiner describes the plan for the three-week preparatory seminar which was about to begin, and outlines the reasons for the republican constitution of the new school (see p 11). The next day he gets straight down to the real work. 'We shall do justice to our task', he says, 'Only if we do not look upon it merely as an intellectual and emotional undertaking, but as a truly moral and spiritual one.'

This means that we cannot rely only on our own unaided strength. 'You will therefore understand if, right at the beginning, we first try to be conscious of the links which we want to forge with the spiritual worlds'. Then comes the challenge. Not just on special occasions but 'as we go about our educational work, we must realise that we are not living only on this physical plane.' We have to shed this deeply entrenched materialist attitude and try to cultivate a continuous awareness of other dimensions. And with this Steiner moves forward to a simple but profound foundation ceremony:

> We would be well-advised at the very beginning of our preparatory work to be aware of the need to create contacts with the spiritual powers at whose behest and under whose mandate each one of us will have to work. I therefore ask you to look upon these introductory words as a kind of prayer addressed to those powers who, working through Imaginations, Inspirations and Intuitions, are to stand behind us as we take on this task.

What followed was an invocation in the form of an imaginative picture of the archetypal pattern of the college of teachers. This *College Imagination* was not written down at the time and was for many years transmitted only by word of mouth. Today, however, it has been placed in the public domain. Several different recollections of Steiner's words exist and the exact form of words cannot now be recovered. But the general picture is clear enough.

It is not only the teachers who are present. Behind each teacher stands a guardian angel who gives the *strength* needed to develop the power of creative imagination essential for living teaching. And we may note that *self-management* is necessary because it ensures that no arbitrary rules and regulations will interfere with this connection.

Circling above the heads of those gathered in the meeting, Steiner says, are archangelic beings From one teacher to another they carry the fruit of experience and open the sources of the inspiration needed for the work. They enable us to develop *courage* and out of this courage they form a chalice. Here we may note that this can only happen if *experiential study* finds the space it needs within the college meetings.

Into this chalice of courage, still higher spiritual beings—the archai—let fall a drop of *light*. Through this they seek to help the teachers develop 'intuition', the quintessential cognition aimed at by spiritual *self-education*. This is crucial because the creative activity required for real teaching is only reliably available when teachers learn how to transform unconscious will into the ability to act consciously.

The spirit of the Waldorf School

Although the details vary, it is clear from all the accounts that Steiner spoke of how the drop of light came from the 'good spirit of our time'. In trying to understand what is meant here it may be important to take account of what Steiner said to the last two monthly assemblies at the end of the school's first year

> There is a spirit that is always meant to prevail here, a spirit that your teachers bring to this place. From the spirit of the cosmos, they learn to bring this spirit here to you; they take in what Saint. Paul said with all of their souls. The spirit of Christ prevails throughout our school; whether we are doing arithmetic, reading, writing, or whatever we do, we do it with the attitude that the Christ awakened in us: 'I am with you always, even unto the end of the world'.
>
> This is the spirit that is meant to prevail here, and it will do so through what your teachers bring to you with love, patience and

endurance. May it also prevail through what lives in your souls! (10.6.20 *Rudolf Steiner in the Waldorf School* p 37)

Alongside everything we have learned here, which the individual teachers have demonstrated so beautifully, there is something else present, something that I would like to call the spirit of the Waldorf School. It is meant to lead us to true piety again.

Basically, it is the spirit of Christianity that wafts through all our rooms, that comes from every teacher and goes out to every child, even when it seems that something very far from religion is being taught, such as arithmetic, for example.

Here it is always the spirit of Christ that comes from the teacher and is to enter the hearts of the children—this spirit that is imbued with love, real human love. (24.7.20 *Rudolf Steiner in the Waldorf School* p 58)

It was not until 1923, shortly after handing over the *Offering Service,* that Steiner returned to this theme in detail. Speaking of 'the living spirit which has to pervade Waldorf pedagogy' he stresses that,

One has to have the good will to want to know it from all sides, and one must never be satisfied with having grasped one particular aspect of it. As a Waldorf teacher, one has to be conscious of having to widen and deepen one's knowledge more and more, instead of feeling satisfied with one's achievements, thinking that one is, after all, quite a clever fellow. If one has lived one's way into Waldorf pedagogy, one will soon get over such delusions! For a true Waldorf teacher, everything that flows from it has to be imbued with true heart and soul forces. It has to spring from the right kind of self-confidence, which rests upon one's trust in God.

If one is aware of the divine forces working within, one will be fed by an ever-flowing fount of life, flowing since time immemorial—quite apart from what one may or may not have learnt outwardly. One is only at the beginning of the way if one's self-confidence stems from outer achievements. One is where one ought to be when self-confidence has led to confidence in the working of God—when it has led to the awareness of the power of the words: 'Not I, but the Christ in me'. But when this happens, self-confidence becomes at the same time self-modesty, because one knows that divinely

> Christian forces are reflected in what is carried in one's soul. It is this spirit that has to reign throughout the school.
>
> If it were lacking, the school would be like an organism in outer nature from which lifeblood was being drawn, or which was being slowly asphyxiated. It is this spirit which matters above all. And if it is alive, it will engender enthusiasm, irrespective of the personnel or the leadership of the school.
>
> And then one can also have confidence that something of an objective spirit will live throughout the school, which is not the same as the accumulation of each teacher's individual spirit. This, however, can be nurtured only gradually within the life of the college of teachers (22.4.23 *Changing Consciousness* pp178–93)

The whole is more than just the sum of the parts. Within every Waldorf school there is—or there should be—a spiritual entity over and above the combined forces of the individual teachers:

> There certainly exists—and these things have to be said in our days—a spirit of our Waldorf School in Stuttgart which is independent of the existing body of teachers and into which these teachers have to live. It becomes ever clearer that under certain circumstances one or the other teacher may be more or less capable—but this spirit of the school has its own life. (12.10.21 *GA* 339)

And a school will thrive to the extent that members of the college of teachers learn to be actively aware of this spirit.

The spiritual quick with life

On one of his last visits to the school, Steiner reiterated the need constantly to invoke the presence of the spiritual helpers of the school (19.6.24 *Education for Adolescence* p 107))

> As each new school year comes round . . . I wish that what I have to say . . . may always have something of the character of a prayer, of a turning in prayer to the spiritual, invoking its presence among us—not merely the spiritual in its intellectual aspect, but the spiritual that is quick with life.
>
> May you indeed be conscious of its presence, spreading itself among us like a cloud of living light and experience, that the spirits themselves are invoked by what we discuss when we meet like this at

the beginning of a new year. That our words reach them and that they are present to hear our appeal: Help us, enliven our work through your spiritual presence; let it flow into our souls and into our hearts, that we may carry on our work in the right way.

If you can feel this, if you can grasp as a living experience what we want to place at the beginning of our new school year, then you will perceive for yourselves the aim and purpose that has been with me throughout this course. And so I would like to place here at the conclusion of our work together the following short meditation

We have the will to work
That into all our work may flow,
That which, out of the spiritual world,
Working in soul and spirit,
In life and body,
Strives to be human within us.

Part 6 A Republic presupposes Self-Education

As one studies what Steiner has to say about the college of teachers being a republican academy—that is, a body of free teachers freely co-operating in an on-going teacher training seminar—one gradually begins to realise that for Steiner a republican school presupposes a formidable self-education on the part of its members.

This can be daunting. We may not find it easy to accept that our education is never finished. That we can always learn from the experience of others, even those much less experienced than ourselves. But this was something Steiner stressed from the very beginning of the Waldorf school movement. During May 1919, some three months before the first meeting of the future college of teachers, Steiner gave three lectures in Stuttgart on *A Social Basis for Education.* Again and again he returns to the economic and political chaos of the post-war era and insists that its origin lies in a failure to educate children adequately. Part of the problem he identifies is an ever-narrowing specialisation:

> People have become accustomed to this without ever getting beyond what they have absorbed as knowledge at school, considering this as an end in itself, whereas the important thing is *learning to learn.* Learning to learn, so that, however old one is, one can remain, up to

> the very year of one's death, a student of life. Today even when people have taken their degree, as a rule they have exhausted their powers of learning by the time they are out of their twenties. They are unable to learn anything more from life; parrot-wise they reel off what they have absorbed up to then. At most they have, now and again, an inkling of what is going on. Those who are different are exceptional.
>
> It is important that we discover an educational method where people learn to learn, and go on learning from life their whole life long. There is nothing in life from which we cannot learn. We should have different ground beneath our feet today if people had learnt how to learn. (18.5.19 *Social Basis* p 30)

Because the person who has learned *how* to learn has the possibility of continuing self-education or, as the French put it, *éducation permanente.*

And those who recognise that a successful republic presupposes self-education may feel lonely as well. For a college of teachers may contain few who share that view of the situation. But Steiner tells us that if the right spirit is alive, 'it will engender enthusiasm, irrespective of the personnel or the leadership of the school'. So although we may feel isolated and depressed by what takes place in college meetings, Steiner urges us to ask ourselves, 'What must *I* do, damn it, to make things better next time?'

What must I do, damn it?

And what can we do? Individually we must attempt to shift our consciousness to a higher level. Because collectively we need to be able to collaborate with the utmost level of consciousness we can muster.

So our first task as we sit in the meeting must be to build the college itself. Not of course the physical place in which we meet, although that matters too. What we build is the meeting's subtle form and how we do it, and whether we do it consciously, makes a difference to the life of the school as a whole. Wakefulness and active listening are what is required. 'Stop sleep-walking through the meetings', Steiner implores us. 'Wake up!'

Wakefulness is staying centred and focused on the matter in hand. Wakeful members of a college are in a position to practise active listening. Inwardly engaging with what is being said but restraining any urge to vocalise their immediate reactions. Inwardly seeking for a true picture of the situation, an image or parable which sheds light on the question. Actively listening for the possibility of real inspiration to enter the situation—fresh ideas, new possibilities, reconciliations. Speaking rarely; concisely; to the point; and advancing the group's understanding of the matter in hand.

A true college of teachers does not exist simply because a group of teachers meet regularly under that banner. Steiner tells us that when personal antipathies start to erupt into discussions 'you could not say that there exists even the very first beginnings of a college of teachers'. *A true college starts to exist only where there is social harmony.*

By the same token, a true college of teachers only starts to exist *when a significant proportion of those present are awake and listening actively.* And its existence can fade if people become tired and cease actively to support a healthy process.

Thirdly, a true college of teachers does not exist where management issues crowd out discussion of how best to educate the children. It only starts to exist *when how to educate the children is the primary focus of the work*

The emancipation of education

Steiner's view of the college of teachers is a challenging ideal. But however imperfectly realised, it has proved a fertile influence: the many hundreds of Waldorf schools, in many different countries, form much the largest grouping of non-hierarchical organisations in the world. They have been an important laboratory of experiment with new social forms. And with all their failings there is a wealth of experience of how to work without bosses.

In *Towards Social Renewal* Steiner maintained that all of education should be organised like this. The Waldorf teachers were urged to recognise the need for compromises (p11) but on the fundamental principles Steiner is completely uncompromising. He held that political influence in education is a severe misfortune because the evolution of human society misses its full potential as long as human creativity is stunted and inhibited by authoritarian social forms. Much talent will continue to be wasted until education becomes self-governing and teachers are free to work more creatively.

> Human culture has matured toward freedom within the framework of the state. But it cannot exercise this freedom without complete autonomy of action. The nature which spiritual life has assumed requires that it constitutes a fully autonomous member of the social organism. The administration of education, from which all culture develops, must be turned over to the educators. Both economic and political considerations should be entirely excluded from

this administration. Each teacher should arrange his or her time so that he can also be an administrator in his field. He should be just as much at home attending to administrative matters as he is in the classroom.

No-one should make decisions who is not directly engaged in the educational process. No parliament or congress, nor any individual who was perhaps *once* an educator, is to have anything to say. What is experienced in the teaching process would then flow naturally into the administration.

The possible advantages of a constitutional separation of education and politics have attracted only limited interest during the twentieth century. It is true that in recent years some countries (eg France) have reduced national control of school curriculum; while others (eg Britain) have sharply curtailed the role local government plays in running schools. And although still in essence monarchical, the management of schools has moved some way towards a more participative style.

But self-managing schools without head-teachers? Local, national and international co-ordination without state educational bureaucracies? Steiner's call for the *emancipation* of education is scarcely ever heard within the mainstream of educational discussion.

Although Steiner eventually realised that the full emancipation of education would be a long and arduous struggle, he remained hopeful that the Waldorf school movement would never lose sight of the eventual goal. Speaking to the college of teachers at the beginning of the sixth year of the first Waldorf School he states

> It is ever again my earnest desire that the year of work before us be permeated with a sense of the greatness of our task and with the inner experience that in the fulfilment of our task we are, in all humility, missionaries for the evolution of mankind. (19.6.24 *Education for Adolescence)*

The need to develop teamwork skills.

But missionaries need to keep up to date. We do well to remember that Steiner urged teachers to be interested in all aspects of the modern world. We need to ensure that our understanding of how best to work as a college of teachers takes into account every useful insight, whatever its origin.

In particular there is a whole body of twentieth century research into group dynamics which contains real pearls as well as many empty oysters. A brief study of elementary meeting skills can be invaluable. Many groups could learn a lot about how to stop avoiding teamwork if they took the time to work with Wilfred Bion's discoveries about the primitive emotions of groups. There is much else that deserves close attention.

And there is useful guidance nearer home. All colleges could profit from working with Marjory Spock's helpful exposition of Goethean conversation. Many might make progress through considering the recommendation of Georg Kuhlewind that meditation together should find a place in college meetings. Much that stems from the work of Bernard Lievegoed can also help us to become more effective republicans.

Freedom, aesthetic education and the 'republican academy'

In its pure form the republican academy envisaged by Rudolf Steiner is a rare harvest that seldom endures for long.

Steiner often acknowledged the philosophy of the poet Schiller as an important influence. Especially the undeservedly neglected *Letters on Aesthetic Education* of 1795 in which Schiller argues that without an artistic education real human freedom is impossible; yet communities based on aesthetic education are hard to find:

> We are likely to find . . . the pure republic only in some few chosen circles, where conduct is governed, not by some soulless imitation of the manners and morals of others, but by the aesthetic nature we have made our own; where men make their way, with undismayed simplicity and tranquil innocence, through even the most involved and complex situations, free alike of the compulsion to infringe the freedom of others in order to assert their own, as of the necessity to shed their dignity in order to manifest grace. (Letter 27)

But we should not let the best be the enemy of the good. When Schiller broke through to an understanding of why artistic education nurtures human freedom he was unable to put forward a practical means of realising his ideal. It was Steiner who first saw how this radiant vision needs to be anchored in an efficacious psychology of child development

> A real permeation by social art of our community through education would give us a true culture of the will. For no-one can have will

> who has not had it drawn out by a genuinely artistic education. To realise this secret of the connection between art and life—especially with the will element in man—is one of the very first requirements of future psychological education; and in future all education must be psychological. (Stuttgart 1.6.19 *Social Basis)*

Schiller correctly foresaw that it would be at least a century before the implications of his discoveries would have much practical effect. But now that a further century has passed the Waldorf school movement carries forward nearly eighty years of practical experience of self-managing aesthetic education.

In the twenty-first century alternatives to the authoritarian social forms still predominant in the so-called 'democracies' of the industrialised world will be sought with increasing urgency.

The experience of Waldorf education has much to offer the search for new forms of social organisation that liberate human creativity. But a really effective contribution to a wider movement for social change will depend on the Waldorf school movement developing a much firmer grasp of why teachers cannot be free to work creatively without republican self-management, experiential study and continuing self-education.

Bibliography

Works by Rudolf Steiner *(short titles in bold)*

Changing Consciousness: *The Child's Changing Consciousness and Waldorf Education* (Anthroposophic Press, 1996). (GA306).

Conferences. *Conferences with Teachers* (Steiner Schools Fellowship, 1986, 1987, 1988, 1989).

Deeper Insights: *Deeper Insights into Education* (Anthroposophic Press, 1988). (GA3O2a).

Education and Anthroposophy: *Waldorf Education and Anthroposophy* I (Anthroposophic Press, 1995). (GA304).

Education for Adolescence: *Waldorf Education for Adolescence. High School Education* (Anthroposophic Press, 1996). (GA 302).

Human Values: *Human Values in Education* (Rudolf Steiner Press, 1971). (GA 310).

The Kingdom of Childhood: *The Kingdom of Childhood* (Anthroposophic Press, 1995). (GA 311)

Knowledge of the Higher Worlds. (Rudolf Steiner Press, 1966) (GA??)

Modern Art: *A Modern Art of Education* (Rudolf Steiner Press, 1981) (GA 307).

Rudolf Steiner in the Waldorf School*—Lectures and Conversations,* Anthroposophic Press, 1996 (GA 298).

Social Basis: *A Social Basis for Education* (Rudolf Steiner Schools Fellowship, 1994) (GA 192)

Spiritual Foundation: *The Spiritual Ground of Education* (Garber Publications, n.d.). (GA 305).

Study of Man: *The Study of Man* (Rudolf Steiner Press, London, 2nd edition 1966) A recent retranslation is *Foundations of Human Experience* Anthroposophic Press, 1996). (GA 293)

Towards Social Renewal (Rudolf Steiner Press 1976)

Works by other authors

Wilfred Bion, *Experiences in Groups* (Routledge, 1990)

Ernst Lehrs, *Republican, not Democratic* (St George Publications, Spring Valley, New York, 1981)

Friedrich Schiller, *On the Aesthetic Education of Man in a series of Letters (ed E M Wilkinson and LA Willoughby* (Oxford University Press, 1967)

Marjory Spock, *The Art of Goethean Coversation* (St George Publications, Spring Valley, New York, 1983)